Oxford
First
Rhyming
Dictionary

OXFORD
UNIVERSITY PRESS

Great Clarendon Street, Oxford OX2 6DP

Oxford University Press is a department of the University of Oxford.
It furthers the University's objective of excellence in research, scholarship,
and education by publishing worldwide in

Oxford   New York

Auckland   Cape Town   Dar es Salaam   Hong Kong   Karachi
Kuala Lumpur   Madrid   Melbourne   Mexico City   Nairobi
New Delhi   Shanghai   Taipei   Toronto

With offices in

Argentina   Austria   Brazil   Chile   Czech Republic   France   Greece
Guatemala   Hungary   Italy   Japan   Poland   Portugal   Singapore
South Korea   Switzerland   Thailand   Turkey   Ukraine   Vietnam

Oxford is a registered trade mark of Oxford University Press
in the UK and in certain other countries

Text © John Foster 2003
Illustrations by Katie Saunders and Charlotte Canty © Oxford University Press 2003
Illustrations by Mary McQuillan © Mary McQuillan 2003
Database right Oxford University Press (maker)

First published 2003
This edition 2008

British Library Cataloguing in Publication Data available

ISBN: 978 0 19 911682 9 paperback
3 5 7 9 10 8 6 4
ISBN: 978 0 19 911872 4 hardback
1 3 5 7 9 10 8 6 4 2
ISBN: 978 0 19 911220 3 big book
1 3 5 7 9 10 8 6 4 2

Designed by Melissa Orrom Swan

Printed in Malaysia by Imago (paperback)
Printed in China (big book)

Paper used in the production of this book is a natural, recyclable product made from wood
grown in sustainable forests. The manufacturing process conforms to the environmental
regulations of the country of origin.

www.schooldictionaries.co.uk

Oxford
First
Rhyming
Dictionary

John Foster
with illustrations by
Mary McQuillan, Katie Saunders & Charlotte Canty

OXFORD
UNIVERSITY PRESS

How to use this dictionary

You can use this dictionary to help you to find words that rhyme.

You can also use it to learn how to spell words that belong to the same rhyming family.

The alphabet

The key words in this dictionary are listed in alphabetical order. Find your way around the dictionary and the word you are looking for by using the alphabet down the side of each page.

Key words

A key word is a word you use very often. In this dictionary, the key words are in red. Look up the key word to find other words that rhyme with it.

Rhyme family

A rhyme family is a group of words that end with the same rhyming sound and have the same spelling pattern.

You will find the rhyming sound after the key word.

Example:

key word   **rhyming sound**

breeze   *-eeze*

rhyme family

freeze   sneeze   wheeze

Sometimes there are several words from one rhyme family which rhyme with words from another rhyme family.

Example:

-eeze rhymes with -ees
bees chimpanzees   knees   trees

And sometimes there are words that rhyme with the key word but have a different spelling pattern.

Example:

Other words that rhyme with breeze
cheese   these   fleas   teas   please

Rhymes

There are lots of rhymes throughout the dictionary. Use them as a starting point to write rhymes of your own!

> Stan, Stan, the lollipop man
> Drives a blue and yellow van
> And washes his socks in a frying pan.

Indexes

This dictionary has two indexes. The A–Z Index on page 68 lists every word in this dictionary. The key words are printed in **bold** type. This index will lead you to the page where you will find the rhyming words you are looking for.

The Index of Rhyming Sounds on page 78 lists every rhyming sound in this dictionary. You can look up the sound that you want to make rhymes with and go straight to the key word in the main part of the book.

These are the features of the dictionary:

capital letter

letter

rhyming sound

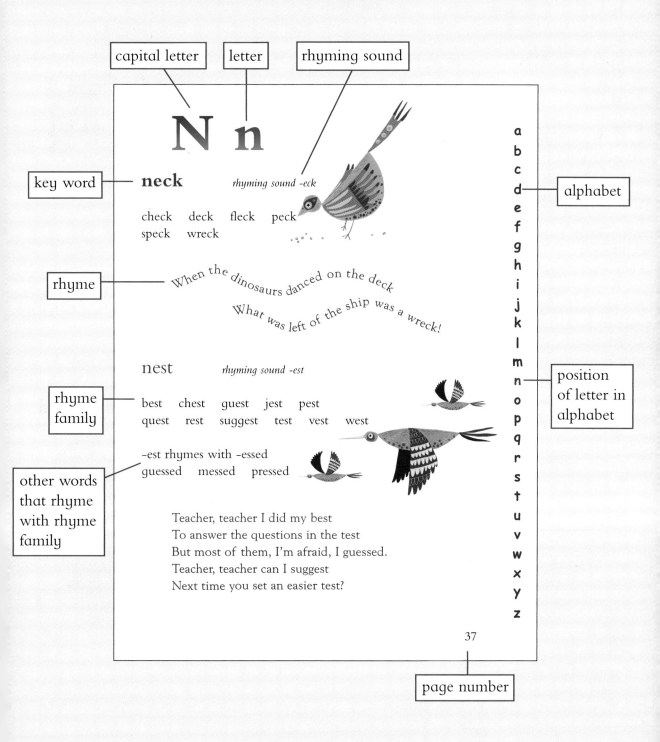

N n

neck   *rhyming sound -eck*

check   deck   fleck   peck
speck   wreck

key word

alphabet

rhyme

When the dinosaurs danced on the deck
What was left of the ship was a wreck!

nest   *rhyming sound -est*

best   chest   guest   jest   pest
quest   rest   suggest   test   vest   west

rhyme family

position of letter in alphabet

-est rhymes with -essed
guessed   messed   pressed

other words that rhyme with rhyme family

Teacher, teacher I did my best
To answer the questions in the test
But most of them, I'm afraid, I guessed.
Teacher, teacher can I suggest
Next time you set an easier test?

a
b
c
d
e
f
g
h
i
j
k
l
m
n
o
p
q
r
s
t
u
v
w
x
y
z

37

page number

A a

ape   *rhyming sound -ape*

cape   escape   grape   scrape
shape   tape

An ape in a cape
Has made an escape from the zoo.
If you see an ape in a cape
We'd like to hear from you.

arm   *rhyming sound -arm*

alarm   charm   farm
harm

-arm rhymes with -alm
calm palm

B b

back *rhyming sound -ack*

black   crack   Jack   pack   quack   rack   sack
smack   snack   stack   track

There was a young fellow called Jack
Who jumped on a donkey's back
   When he gave it a smack
   It reared its back
And tossed Jack onto the track.

bag *rhyming sound -ag*

brag   crag   drag   flag   nag   rag
sag   snag   stag   tag   wag

When Mum picks up her bag
   Our dog's tail starts to wag
      Back and forth like a flag.

9

ball   *rhyming sound -all*

all   call   fall   football
hall   small   stall   tall   wall

-all rhymes with -awl
crawl   scrawl   sprawl

I spent hours kicking a ball
At a goal that was drawn on a wall
Without scoring a goal at all
'Cause the goal on the wall was too small!

bang   *rhyming sound -ang*

clang   fang   gang   hang
rang   sang   sprang   tang   twang

bed

rhyming sound -ed

bled   fed   fled   led
red   shed   sled   Ted   wed

-ed rhymes with some -ead words
bread   dead   head   lead   read
spread   thread   tread

Another word that rhymes with bed is
said

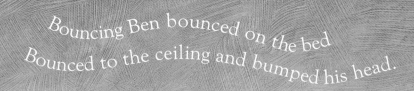

Bouncing Ben bounced on the bed
Bounced to the ceiling and bumped his head.

a
b
c
d
e
f
g
h
i
j
k
l
m
n
o
p
q
r
s
t
u
v
w
x
y
z

boat *rhyming sound -oat*

coat   float   gloat   goat   moat
oat   throat

-oat rhymes with -ote
note   vote   wrote

book *rhyming sound -ook*

brook   cook   crook   hook   look
rook   shook   took

breeze *rhyming sound -eeze*

freeze   sneeze   wheeze

-eeze rhymes with -ees
bees   chimpanzees   knees   trees

Other words that rhyme with breeze
cheese   these   fleas   teas   please

Chimpanzees sit up in trees
Picking fleas from off their knees.

C c

cage *rhyming sound -age*

age   page   rage   stage   wage

cake *rhyming sound -ake*

bake   brake   fake   flake   lake
make   mistake   quake   rake
shake   snake   stake   take   wake

Some –eak words rhyme with cake
break   steak

camp *rhyming sound -amp*

champ   clamp   cramp   damp   lamp
ramp   scamp   stamp   tramp

a
b
c
d
e
f
g
h
i
j
k
l
m
n
o
p
q
r
s
t
u
v
w
x
y
z

a
b
c
d
e
f
g
h
i
j
k
l
m
n
o
p
q
r
s
t
u
v
w
x
y
z

car   *rhyming sound -ar*

bar   far   guitar   jar   scar
spar   star   tar

Other words that rhyme with car
pa   ma   are

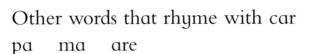

★ I want to be a TV star.
I want to be a TV star!
I want to play a flash guitar.
I want to drive a racing car.
I want to be the best by far.
I want to be a TV star!

chip   *rhyming sound -ip*

clip   dip   drip   flip   grip
hip   lip   nip   pip   rip   sip
ship   skip   slip   snip   strip
trip   whip   zip   *tip*

14

clock

rhyming sound -ock

block   dock   flock   frock   knock
lock   rock   shock   sock

Knock knock! What a shock!
    Look at the clock - eight o'clock!
Grab your vest. Grab your frock.
    Grab your shoe. Grab your sock.
Slam the door. Lock the lock.
    Hurry! Hurry! Round the block.
Get to school by nine o'clock.
    What a morning! What a shock!
If you don't get up at Mum's first knock.

cow

rhyming sound -ow

allow   bow   brow   how   now
row   wow

cup

rhyming sound -up

pup   sup   up

D d

dad   *rhyming sound -ad*

bad   glad   had   lad   mad
pad   sad

Another word that rhymes with dad is
add

dog   *rhyming sound -og*

bog   cog   flog   fog   frog
hog   jog   log

I tripped over my dog in the fog.
I fell into a bog and frightened a frog.

dream *rhyming sound -eam*

beam   cream   scream   steam
stream   team

-eam rhymes with -eem
seem

I scream. We all scream.

It's snowing It's snowing, It's snowing It's snowing, ice cream.

17

dress   *rhyming sound -ess*

address   bless   chess   guess   less   mess
press   stress

I've made a mess. I've made a mess.
I've spilt my drink all down my dress.
It'll need a clean. It'll need a press.
I've made a mess. I've spoiled my dress.

duck   *rhyming sound -uck*

buck   chuck   cluck   luck   muck
pluck   struck   stuck   suck   truck   yuck

E e

ear   *rhyming sound -ear*

clear   dear   fear   gear   hear   near   tear

-ear rhymes with -eer
beer   cheer   deer

Other words that rhyme with ear
here   pier

Oh dear, I can't hear.
You're not very clear.
You'll have to come near.
I fear that I've got
A flea in my ear!

end   *rhyming sound -end*

bend   blend   friend   lend   mend
pretend   send   spend   tend   trend

I'm at my wit's end with my friend.
Whenever we play "Let's pretend"
She wants to be boss.
It makes me so cross.
It's driving me round the bend.

F f

face *rhyming sound -ace*

ace   Grace   lace   pace   place
space   trace   race

I took my place beside Grace
At the start of the three-legged race
   But my lace came undone
   When we started to run
And Grace fell flat on her face!

a
b
c
d
e
f
g
h
i
j
k
l
m
n
o
p
q
r
s
t
u
v
w
x
y
z

fish *rhyming sound -ish*

dish   fish   swish   wish

five *rhyming sound -ive*

alive   arrive   dive   drive   hive
jive   live

fox *rhyming sound -ox*

box   ox

-ox rhymes with -ocks
blocks   clocks   docks
flocks   frocks   knocks
locks   rocks
shocks   socks

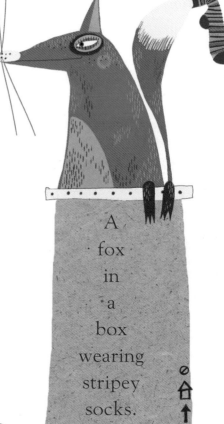

A
fox
in
a
box
wearing
stripey
socks.

G g

game
rhyming sound -ame

blame   came   dame   fame   flame
frame   lame   name   same   shame
tame

gate
rhyming sound -ate

ate   crate   date   fate   hate
Kate   late   mate   plate   rate
skate   slate   state

-ate rhymes with -ait
bait   wait

Other words that rhyme with gate
eight   weight
great   straight   fete

a b c d e f g h i j k l m n o p q r s t u v w x y z

gold *rhyming sound -old*

bold　cold　fold　hold　old
scold　sold　told

Let's play pirates!
I'll be the captain big and bold.
I'm in charge. You do as you're told.
You must give me all your gold.
Then I'll tie you up and throw you in the hold
While I sit in my cabin counting my gold.

grass *rhyming sound -ass*

brass　class　glass　pass

H h

hair   *rhyming sound -air*

air   chair   fair   lair   pair   stair

-air rhymes with -are
bare   beware   care   dare   fare   hare   mare
rare   scare   spare

Other words that rhyme with hair
bear   pear   wear   their
there   where
prayer

hat   *rhyming sound -at*

at   bat   brat   cat   chat   fat
flat   gnat   mat   pat   rat
sat   spat   splat   that

a b c d e f g h i j k l m n o p q r s t u v w x y z

hen   *rhyming sound -en*

Ben   den   Ken   Len   pen
ten   then   when

Another word that rhymes with hen is
again

There were two men called Ben and Ken.
Ben had a pig. Ken had a hen.
Ben swapped his pig for Ken's hen.
Then they swapped them back again
Again, again, again and again.
Now who's got the hen, Ben or Ken?

hill   *rhyming sound -ill*

bill   chill   drill   fill   grill   ill   Jill   kill
mill   pill   skill   spill   still   thrill   till   will

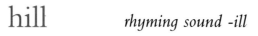

Jack and Jill went up the hill. "Wait there, Jack," said Jill.
Jill ran off down the hill. And Jack is up there still!

26

hole

rhyming sound -ole

mole   pole   role   stole   vole   whole

-ole rhymes with -oal
foal   goal

Other words that rhyme with hole
bowl   roll   stroll   troll

Beneath the bridge is a deep, dark hole
In which there lives a terrible troll.

hut

rhyming sound -ut

but   cut   gut   jut   nut
rut   shut   strut

I i

ice *rhyming sound -ice*

advice   dice   lice   mice   nice   price
rice   slice   spice   twice

Three blind mice didn't listen to advice
Went skating on the pond ...

... and fell ...

... through the ...

... ice.

ink *rhyming sound -ink*

blink   brink   chink   clink   drink
link   mink   pink   rink   shrink   sink
stink   think   wink

J j

jam   *rhyming sound -am*

am   cram   dam   exam   gram
ham   Pam   pram   ram   Sam
scram   slam   swam   tram
wham   yam

Another word that rhymes with jam is
lamb

jug   *rhyming sound -ug*

bug   chug   drug   dug   glug
hug   mug   plug   rug   shrug
slug   smug   snug   thug   tug

Said the slug in the jug
    To the bug in the rug
        "I'm not very snug in this jug.
            Are you snug in your rug?"
                "I am," said the bug, feeling smug.

a
b
c
d
e
f
g
h
i
j
k
l
m
n
o
p
q
r
s
t
u
v
w
x
y
z

jump

rhyming sound -ump

bump clump dump hump lump
plump pump slump stump thump

I tried to jump on a camel's hump.
Now I have a big lump
'Cause I fell on the ground with a thump!

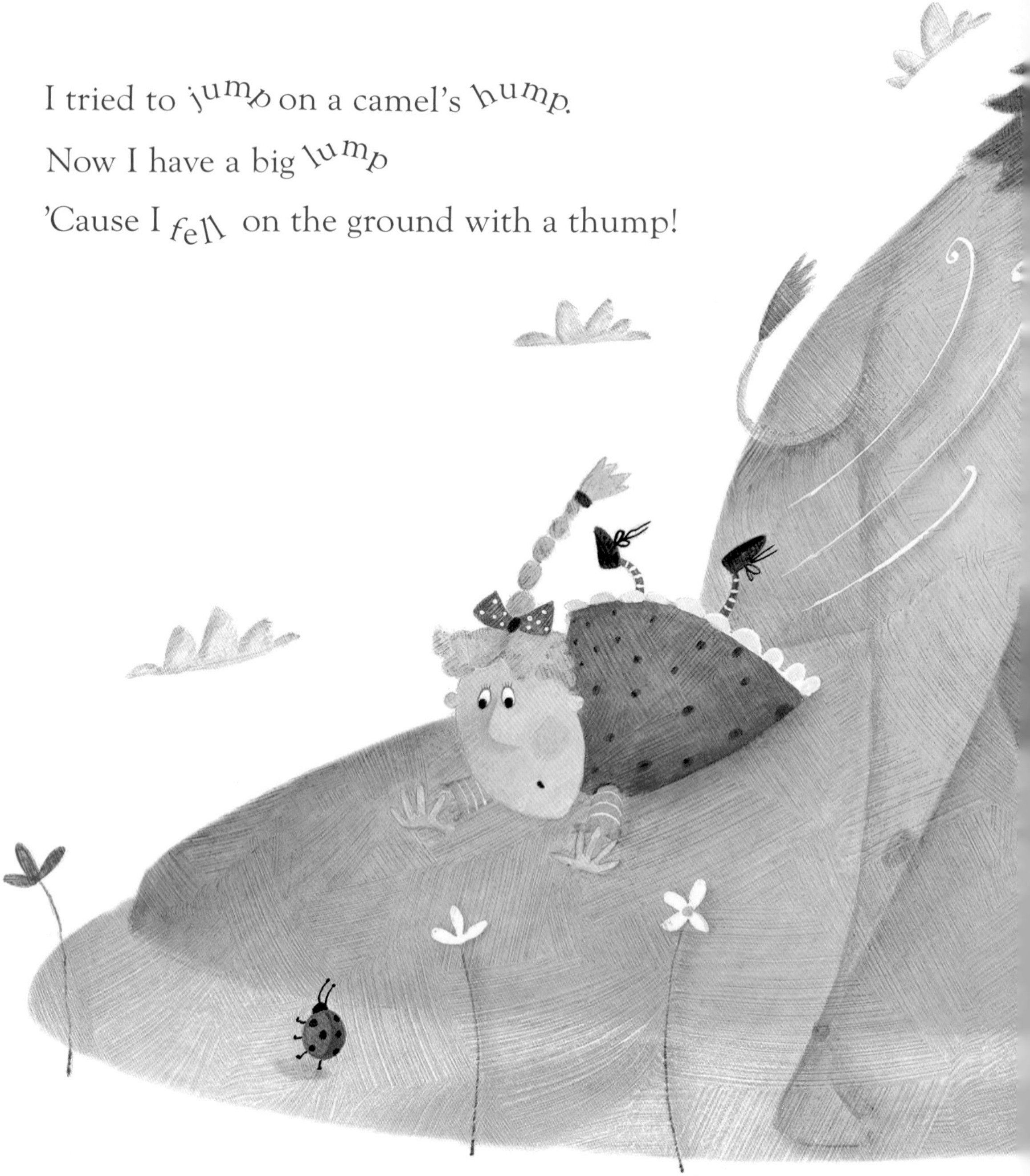

a
b
c
d
e
f
g
h
i
j
k
l
m
n
o
p
q
r
s
t
u
v
w
x
y
z

31

K k

kick   *rhyming sound -ick*

brick   chick   click   flick   lick   pick
quick   sick   stick   thick   tick   trick

Lick
a lolly
on a
stick!
Lick it
fast! Lick
It
quick!

king   *rhyming sound -ing*

bring   cling   ding   ping   ring
sing   spring   sting   string   swing
thing   wing

If I had a magic ring
I could wish for anything:
To swing on a star on a silver string
To dance with fairies in the spring
To sing and fly like a bird on the wing
To live in a palace like a king.

knit   *rhyming sound -it*

bit   exit   fit   flit   grit   hit   kit   lit   pit
sit   slit   spit   split   twit

L l

lid   *rhyming sound -id*

bid   did   forbid   grid   hid   kid
rid   skid   slid

light   *rhyming sound -ite*

bright   fight   flight   fright   knight
might   night   right   sight   tight

-ight rhymes with -ite
bite   kite   quite   white   write

lunch   *rhyming sound -unch*

bunch   crunch   hunch   munch   punch
scrunch

There's a rabbit in the dinner queue
    So I've got a hunch
        We'll have a bunch of carrots
            To munch for our lunch.

a
b
c
d
e
f
g
h
i
j
k
l
m
n
o
p
q
r
s
t
u
v
w
x
y
z

M m

map   *rhyming sound -ap*

bap   cap   chap   clap   flap
gap   lap   nap   rap   sap
scrap   slap   snap   strap   tap
trap   wrap   yap   zap

match   *rhyming sound -atch*

batch   catch   hatch   latch   patch
scratch   snatch

meat   *rhyming sound -eat*

beat   bleat   cheat   eat   feat
heat   neat   seat   treat   wheat

-eat rhymes with -eet
feet   greet   meet
sheet   street   sweet

moon

rhyming sound -oon

afternoon   baboon   balloon
cartoon   noon   soon   spoon

-oon rhymes with –une
June   tune

A
baboon flew
up to the moon.
"Go away!" said the
Man in the Moon
And he burst
the baboon's
balloon.

a
b
c
d
e
f
g
h
i
j
k
l
m
n
o
p
q
r
s
t
u
v
w
x
y
z

mud *rhyming sound -ud*

bud   cud   dud   spud   stud   sud   thud

Other words that rhyme with mud
blood   flood

> After the storm there was a flood.
> I went in the garden and played in the mud.
> I got mud in my pants. I got mud in my hair.
> I got myself muddy everywhere.

mum *rhyming sound -um*

drum   gum   glum   plum   strum
sum   yum

Other words that rhyme with mum
crumb   dumb   numb
thumb   come
some

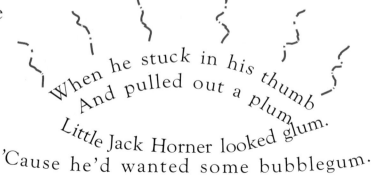

When he stuck in his thumb
And pulled out a plum
Little Jack Horner looked glum.
'Cause he'd wanted some bubblegum.

N n

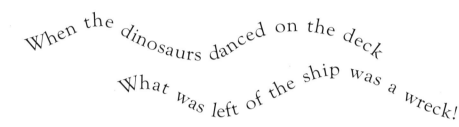

neck   *rhyming sound -eck*

check   deck   fleck   peck
speck   wreck

When the dinosaurs danced on the deck
What was left of the ship was a wreck!

nest   *rhyming sound -est*

best   chest   guest   jest   pest
quest   rest   suggest   test   vest   west

-est rhymes with -essed
guessed   messed   pressed

Teacher, teacher I did my best
To answer the questions in the test
But most of them, I'm afraid, I guessed.
Teacher, teacher can I suggest
Next time you set an easier test?

net   *rhyming sound -et*

bet   forget   fret   get   jet   let   met   pet
set   upset   vet   wet   yet

Other words that rhyme with net
sweat   threat

My dragon came out in a sweat
So I took him to see the vet.
When he saw the vet
He got really upset.
He took off like a jet
And hasn't come back yet.

nine   *rhyming sound -ine*

dine   fine   line   mine   pine   shine
spine   whine   wine

nose   *rhyming sound -ose*

chose   close   hose   pose   those

-ose rhymes with -ows
blows   bows   crows   flows   glows   grows   knows
mows   rows   shows   slows   snows   throws   tows

Other words that rhyme with nose
doze   froze
goes   hoes   toes
sews

The snowman says:
I like it when the north wind blows
And it snows and it freezes
My nose and my toes.

a
b
c
d
e
f
g
h
i
j
k
l
m
n
o
p
q
r
s
t
u
v
w
x
y
z

O o

oil *rhyming sound -oil*

boil   coil   foil   soil   spoil

out *rhyming sound -out*

about   scout   shout   snout   sprout
stout   trout

P p

park

rhyming sound -ark

ark   bark   dark   hark   lark   mark   shark   spark

If you go for a walk in the park after dark
You can hear the ghost dogs bark.

pin

rhyming sound -in

bin   chin   din   fin   grin   in   robin   shin
skin   sin   thin   tin   twin   win

pool

rhyming sound -ool

cool   fool   school   stool   tool

-ool rhymes with –ule
mule   rule

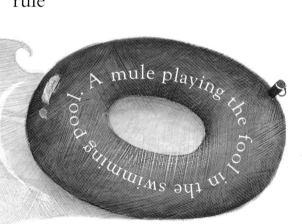

A mule playing the fool in the swimming pool.

pot   *rhyming sound -ot*

blot   cot   dot   forgot   got
hot   jot   knot   lot   not
plot   rot   Scot   shot
spot   tot   trot

pull   *rhyming sound -ull*

bull   full

Another word that rhymes with pull is
wool

How now, brown cow
What's that you pull?
Is it a wagon full of finest wool?

No, it's full of turnips
and I'm a **bull!**

Q q

queen

rhyming sound -een

been green keen
screen seen

-een rhymes with -ean
bean clean Jean
lean mean

Jean, Jean dressed in green
Jean, Jean where have you been?
I've been up to London to visit the
queen.

Jean, Jean dressed in green
Was that you on the TV screen?
Yes it was! It was me with the queen!

a
b
c
d
e
f
g
h
i
j
k
l
m
n
o
p
q
r
s
t
u
v
w
x
y
z

R r

ride   *rhyming sound -ide*

bride   glide   guide   hide   side
slide   tide   wide

-ide rhymes with -ied
cried   died   dried   fried
lied   spied   tied   tried

room   *rhyming sound -oom*

bloom   boom   broom   doom
gloom   groom   loom   zoom

Zoom round the room. **Flash!**

Crash!

Boom!

Here I go on my supersonic broom!

44

rope   *rhyming sound -ope*

cope   hope   mope   pope   slope

Another word that rhymes with rope is
soap

Slippery soap, slippery soap

You haven't a hope

Of

catching

the

soap.

round   *rhyming sound -ound*

around   bound   found
ground   hound   mound
pound   sound   wound

S s

sand   *rhyming sound -and*

band   grand   hand   land   stand

seed   *rhyming sound -eed*

bleed   feed   need   speed   weed

-eed words rhyme with some -ead words
bead   lead   read

There was a young wizard called Reed
Who planted a new type of seed.
He chanted a spell to make it grow well
And it grew and it grew at great speed.
It grew tall as a tower, and gave him great power.
He had grown a magical weed.

sheep

rhyming sound -eep

beep   bleep   cheep   creep   deep   jeep
keep   peep   sleep   steep   sweep   weep

-eep rhymes with -eap
cheap   heap   leap

> At night when everyone's fast asleep
> Out from their cellars, dark and deep
> The goblins creep.

shirt

rhyming sound -irt

dirt   skirt   squirt

-irt rhymes with -urt
hurt   spurt

shop

rhyming sound -op

chop   clop   drop   flop   hop
mop   pop   plop   stop   top

Don't
drop your
l o l l i p o p
Or your lolly
will go
p
l
o
p!

a
b
c
d
e
f
g
h
i
j
k
l
m
n
o
p
q
r
s
t
u
v
w
x
y
z

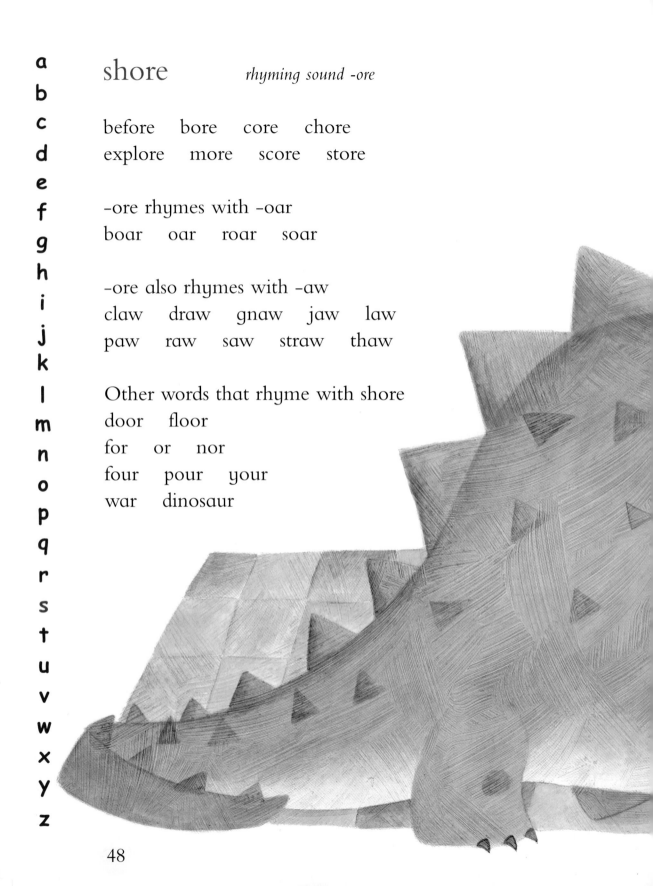

shore   *rhyming sound -ore*

before   bore   core   chore
explore   more   score   store

-ore rhymes with -oar
boar   oar   roar   soar

-ore also rhymes with -aw
claw   draw   gnaw   jaw   law
paw   raw   saw   straw   thaw

Other words that rhyme with shore
door   floor
for   or   nor
four   pour   your
war   dinosaur

Dinah Shore dreamed she saw a dinosaur
Knock on her window with its claw.
Dinah Shore dreamed she saw a dinosaur
Peeping round her bedroom door.
Dinah Shore dreamed she saw a dinosaur
Fast asleep on the kitchen floor.
Dinah Shore dreamed she saw a dinosaur
Wake up and give a mighty **ROAR!**

a
b
c
d
e
f
g
h
i
j
k
l
m
n
o
p
q
r
s
t
u
v
w
x
y
z

a
b
c
d
e
f
g
h
i
j
k
l
m
n
o
p
q
r
s
t
u
v
w
x
y
z

six   *rhyming sound -ix*

fix   mix

-ix rhymes with -icks
bricks   chicks   clicks   flicks   kicks   licks
picks   pricks   sticks   ticks   tricks

The magician flicks his wand
Clicks his fingers
And out of his empty hat he picks
Six fluffy little chicks.

smile   *rhyming sound -ile*

crocodile   file   mile   pile   stile
tile   vile   while

Beware the smile of the crocodile
What he really wants to do
Is smile while he *is chewing you!*

snow

rhyming sound -ow

below   blow   bow   crow   flow
glow   grow   know   low   pillow
row   shadow   show   slow   sow
throw   window

Other words that rhyme with snow
hoe   Joe   toe   hello
no   radio   so
sew   though

song

rhyming sound -ong

along   bong   dong   gong   long
pong   prong   strong   wrong

Sing along! Sing a song!
Bing! Bang! Bong!
Sing along! Sing a song!
Ding! Dang! Dong!

a
b
c
d
e
f
g
h
i
j
k
l
m
n
o
p
q
r
s
t
u
v
w
x
y
z

spade   *rhyming sound -ade*

blade   fade   lemonade   made
marmalade   shade   trade   wade

-ade rhymes with -aid
afraid   laid   paid   raid

-ade also rhymes with -ayed
played   prayed   stayed

After we played we lay in the shade
    Drinking ICE-ICE-ICE-cold lemonade.

speak   *rhyming sound -eak*

beak   creak   leak   peak   sneak
squeak   weak

-eak rhymes with -eek
leek   peek   seek   week

splash
rhyming sound -ash

ash bash cash clash crash dash flash
gash lash mash rash smash thrash trash

sport
rhyming sound -ort

fort port short sort

-ort rhymes with -aught
caught taught

Other words that rhyme with -ort
fought nought ought thought

sun
rhyming sound -un

bun fun gun nun
run spun

-un rhymes with -one
done none one

-un words rhyme with some -on words
son ton won

a
b
c
d
e
f
g
h
i
j
k
l
m
n
o
p
q
r
s
t
u
v
w
x
y
z

swim   *rhyming sound -im*

brim   dim   grim   him   Jim   Kim
prim   rim   skim   slim   Tim   trim

Slim Jim said to prim Kim
"Can you swim?"
"I can't," said prim Kim.
"But trim Tim can swim.
Can you swim as fast as him, Jim?"
"I can swim," said slim Jim
"But not as fast as trim Tim."

T t

tail *rhyming sound -ail*

fail	frail	hail	jail	mail	nail
pail	rail	sail	snail	trail	wail

-ail rhymes with –ale

dale   gale   male   pale   sale   scale   stale
tale   whale

Dale told a tale
Of how he went for a sail
And caught a whale in a pail.

tank   *rhyming sound -ank*

bank   blank   clank   drank   Frank
plank   sank   shrank   spank   stank   thank

There once was a boy called Frank
    Who was fooling around on a plank.

He fell into a tank

And when he came out he stank!

tent   *rhyming sound -ent*

accident   bent   dent   event   lent
rent   scent   sent   spent   went

tie

rhyming sound -ie

die   lie   pie

-ie rhymes with -y

by   cry   dry   fly   fry   my   shy   sky   sly
spy   sty   try   why

-ie also rhymes with -igh

high   sigh   thigh

Other words that rhyme with -ie

dye   eye   buy   guy
bye   goodbye   I

time

rhyming sound -ime

chime   crime   grime
lime   mime   slime

Other words that rhyme with -ime
climb   rhyme

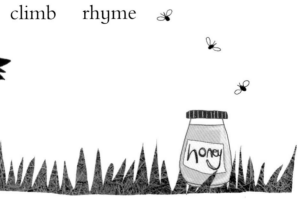

town *rhyming sound -own*

brown   clown   crown   down   drown   frown   gown

A king with a golden crown,
A lady in a fine gown,
And a clown whose trousers have *fallen down!*

toy *rhyming sound -oy*

annoy   boy   enjoy   Roy

train *rhyming sound -ain*

again   brain   chain
drain   gain   main   pain
plain   rain   Spain   stain

-ain rhymes with -ane
cane   crane   Jane   lane
mane   pane   plane

tree *rhyming sound -ee*

bee   flee   free   glee   knee
see   three

Other words that rhyme with –ee
flea   pea   sea   tea
he   me   she   we
chimney   key   monkey

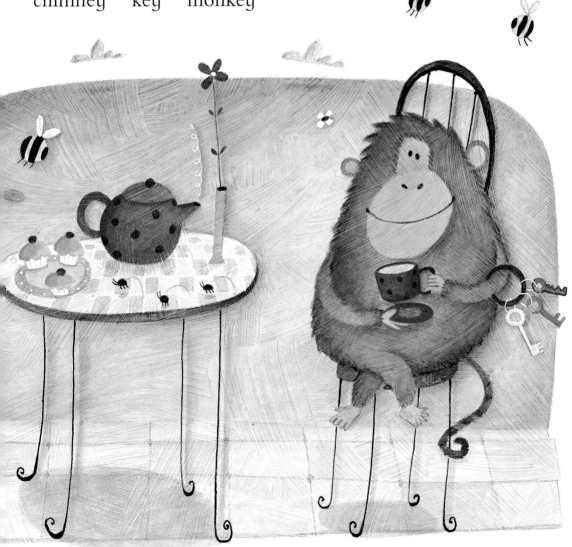

U u

under   *rhyming sound -under*

blunder   thunder

Another word that rhymes with under is
wonder

When thunder booms overhead
My little brother hides under the bed.

V v

van   *rhyming sound -an*

an   can   fan   gran
man   nan   pan   plan
ran   Stan   than

Stan, Stan, the lollipop man
    Drives a blue and yellow van
And washes his socks in a frying pan.

W w

well *rhyming sound -ell*

bell   cell   dwell   fell   hell   sell
shell   spell   smell   tell   unwell   yell

With a yell Doctor Bell tripped and fell
Head first down into the well.
    Now he's lying in bed,
    Holding his head,
Poor Doctor Bell's feeling unwell.

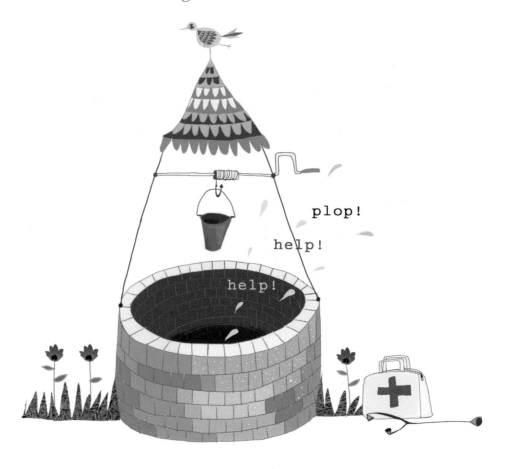

wheel

rhyming sound -eel

eel   feel   heel   kneel   peel
reel   steel

-eel rhymes with -eal
deal   heal   meal   real   seal
squeal   steal

I spin round and round on the Big Wheel. My stomach spins round and round and I feel I'm about to lose my last meal.

I spin round and round on the Big Wheel. My stomach spins round and round and I feel I'm about to lose my last meal.

wig *rhyming sound -ig*

big   dig   fig   jig   pig   rig
swig   twig

A guinea pig
ate a fig while
an earwig danced a jig.

X x

X-ray *rhyming sound -ay*

away   bay   bray   clay   day   hay   hurray
lay   may   pay   play   pray   ray   say   spray
stay   stray   sway   today   tray   way

-ay rhymes with -eigh
neigh   sleigh   weigh

-ay also rhymes with -ey
obey   prey   they

Y y

yard *rhyming sound -ard*

card   hard   lard

Another word that rhymes with yard is
guard

I bought a postcard
of them changing the guard
in the palace yard.

a b c d e f g h i j k l m n o p q r s t u v w x y z

Z z

ZOO   *rhyming sound -oo*

boo   kangaroo   moo

-oo rhymes with -ue
blue   glue   true

-oo also rhymes with -ew
blew   flew   grew   new

Other words that rhyme with zoo
do   to   you   two